HOW GOD BREATHED LIFE INTO ME

LEAH BETH

ISBN 979-8-88540-149-4 (paperback)
ISBN 979-8-88540-150-0 (digital)

Christian Faith Publishing
832 Park Avenue
Meadville, PA 16335
www.christianfaithpublishing.com

Printed in the United States of America

I believe in miracles because I am ONE. And there's no doubt in my mind that the only reason I've made it this far is because God made a way for ME.

CONTENTS

PREFACE

I dedicate this book, my life story, to all my readers. I desire that the words could come forth as *healing oil* poured right on each heart that is hurting and/or searching deeply for love and answers to the whys in your lives. And the blessings from God will come pouring down on each wounded heart and soul as the words of my story are being pondered over.

Many individuals were sent into my life as ministering angels, unaware of what they were doing. Now I want to be that *ministering* angel in your life through my story.

The excitement for me is that one day I will know that my childhood story, though bitter it was, has become the sweetest savor for thousands of people, for you to know that you are not alone. You will get through your hardest trials, and God is sending *you* butterflies to let you know how loved and valued you are.

CHAPTER 1

SUFFERING IN SILENCE

When I was a young girl, I felt totally trapped. I was miserable, unhappy—ugly attitudes. I looked ugly because of the way I felt about myself. No one ever told me I was pretty. I honestly don't ever even remember hearing that word.

I feel led from God to share a few things from my home life. My growing-up years had been so clouded over and filled with bitterness and hatred that I myself even find it hard to fathom. I have read many books, heard many testimonies of people who were in brutal situations and how God brought them out of their horrible mess and changed their lives forever, mostly in troubled divorced homes.

I am now wanting to share from my heart about how things can be in a so-called looking-happy Christian home with both parents present, but yet someone like me—

suffering in such silence that nothing is ever observed or recognized of the misery going on in a child's heart.

I want to be a true blessing for others. I assume there are many people suffering in silence like I did and yet have no idea or just that there *has* to be something terrible wrong with *them*. I want you to know that you are not alone. If God could take someone as ugly and hateful as me and change my whole life, my whole being, and transform me into a totally new person who now has *hope*, where there was ugliness, now peace, love, and joy. Where my heart was hard as a rock, now soft tissue has formed, where I actually have feelings. Wow! You probably say, "Yes, that is right." It is *wow!* over and over and over again.

I wanted nobody to touch me. I would get very angry if anyone tried to give me a hug. I have a beautiful aunt who would try hugging me every time she came over. She was the only person I recall ever actually getting a loving hug from. The other hugs were just a casual hug when family members or relatives would go traveling. I did not appreciate those hugs; to me, they represented all the ugliness and hatred inside of me that I wanted no one to know about.

Because I was not getting love nor did I feel cherished, I only felt duty bound, and it brought heaps of oppression pouring into my life. My dear mother had no idea how to love. I felt totally despised by her. I felt like

I was her worst enemy. I made sure I stayed as far away from her as I could. I recall folding laundry and making neat piles for everyone on the bed or table and carefully putting as many piles in between her pile and mine as I possibly could! I had so much dislike for her that at a very young age, I would go in the enclosed porch right off the kitchen and over and over tell myself, "I hate you. Mom, oh, I hate you!"

Day after day, I did that, thus selling my soul to the devil, and of course having no idea what it was doing to me. I was ten or so when I started and never had a problem telling myself how much I hated her.

One thing I did really enjoy was taking care of the babies as they were born into the home. I would rock them and nurture them. I felt very protective of those dear little souls and yearned to know in my little heart why my mom is so very angry all the time.

Oh, how that weighed on me so heavily. I would watch her daily as she would go about her duties, and she seemed calm and maybe even a little cheerful. Suddenly, out of nowhere, something would tick her off, and she would go into a rage toward one of us children.

I liked to compare her rage to a snake. Those beady eyes would come bulging out, and we would all try to run away and hide. She always caught one of us and would do any harm she could or threaten that Daddy would beat that child when he got home.

And, oh, how I dreaded night time. As we were in bed, I would be pulling my covers over my head, wondering when I will hear those footsteps come up the steps to whip the guilty child. Many times, if not most often, it was I who got whipped. I also got whipped by my mom many times a day.

Guilt and fear were constantly knocking on my scared little heart. I would work so hard to try to please my mom. I remember two compliments she gave me as a child—or ever, I should say. The one time she told me in such a sweet pleasant voice that I was such a good helper to help fold laundry. I was seven years old.

After that I would try to fold laundry with her, close to her to make sure she saw how faithful I was. Instead she would tell me to get out of her way! My little heart would be crushed, and instead of crying or anything, I balled those feelings of rejection up inside of me and would run away before she tried to hit me.

After she told me the compliment, she used that compliment in every way to shame me, to guilt me, to harm me and hurt me in every way possible. She definitely remembered giving me the compliment. She never forgot that even long into my teenage years, into adulthood. That just ate at me like a rat would eat at something they are not allowed to eat. I'm using a rat to compare with since rats only eat what they are not allowed to eat, and they can destroy everything in their path. And that is what the poison was doing to my heart as well, destroying every good thing inside of me and filling my soul and heart with more and more hatred and bitterness.

I loved to read. Any and every book I could get my hands on, I would read. I was not allowed to read, except in the evening or on a Sunday, as we, of course, had a lot of chores to do when we would get home from school. My mind would be filled with the book I was reading, trying to imagine myself being that person, but I felt so bad about myself. I never thought how it would be to be in a family that actually wanted me.

I really and truly thought and always believed that I didn't deserve anything better than I had. I deserved to be a victim. I was supposed to feel this way; if I didn't, I was very prideful. I, of course, didn't know it then, but my mom didn't want me from the day she knew she was pregnant with me. Somehow someone told me that Mom had this dream plan that she was having four children, and they would be four years apart. Well, I came along before my oldest sister wasn't even a year old! We are eleven months apart! Now I understand that all my feelings of rejection started in the womb.

And mom always told me I was born screaming with earache and bellyache, another sign that I was already unhappy and probably didn't want to be born!

Four girls were born into the family in three years! Not anything of mom's wonderful dream family!

CHAPTER 2

BABY SISTER

Only God has the ability to work unspeakable good out of life's tragedies. Grace doesn't depend on suffering to exist, but where there is suffering, we will find God's GRACE available. I am willing to receive it. It is a GIFT that can be rejected or received the same as salvation.

I appreciate these words so much. They are my inspiration I go on daily. I look at my suffering now as a beautiful treasure that I can now open daily and be reminded of where I was and how far I've come. Since I have started writing. It has been bringing many feelings and emotions for me, emotions that I have to look at fair and square, and ask myself, "Okay, have I made peace with this situation?"

And now I feel myself reliving my past! It is very healing. It is helping me look at things deeper in a way that has never entered my mind. I see my mom in a totally different light. Now I have so many questions to ask her, questions that are so deep that my dear mom would probably have no answers for.

I have been seeing my dear mom in a different light since I have had the *love* of *God* in my heart. I had to choose to forgive her, to let go of the ugliness and allow God to fill my heart with good thoughts about my mom, to realize she did the best she really knew how. Since I have done that, I hold no grudges toward her.

Forgiving my mom was the hardest thing that I could ever do. I battled with it as I didn't know that I wanted to forgive my dear mom. I do need to continue with the childhood story and let this part rest for later.

My parents had a four-year baby break after the four daughters were born. There is so little that I remember of my baby sister being born and growing up fast. I do remember her coming to church with us, and I was six years old. I must have been quite feisty. I recall my cousin walking up to my mom and asking if she can hold my little sister. I reached out and bit her finger really hard. I didn't think she should hold her. Her eyes filled with tears, and she jerked her finger away. I remember getting a big scolding from my mom, but I don't recall what happened after that.

My little sister was born during the night. On a Sunday morning, Daddy came to wake us up and said we have a surprise! I went downstairs, wondering what kind of a surprise we could possibly have on a Sunday morning? There was a crib sitting in the kitchen. I peered in it, and in my childlike mind, I'm thinking, *Is it a baby calf?*

Daddy came all smiles and said we have a baby girl! I asked where she came from, and he said she dropped out of heaven—and, yes, I did believe him. Why our parents made us believe that, I will never know.

CHAPTER 3

MOM AND MY OLDEST BROTHER

was eight years old when my brother was born. That time, we had to go away for the night. My dad was so excited to have a little boy! He named him after his dad, who had passed away when he was twelve years old. His mom, my grandma, remained a widow with four young children and never did remarry. She lived to be in her seventies. Daddy was very faithful in helping take care of her needs, always going over to her house, doing things for her.

There is very little that I remember of my little big brother as a baby. Now as I'm writing this, I really do wonder why. What I do remember is that he was a very grouchy little boy. He cried a lot. And I remember hearing mom telling whoever how she doesn't like having a boy. He is so much work and so much more bother than a baby girl. I honestly don't recall her ever being nice to him.

Unknowingly, this put some fear into me to stay away from him. And my dad? It seems to me that he stayed out of the picture completely.

My brother didn't crawl like a child normally does; he scooted around on his bottom. He didn't start walking till he was sixteen months old. When he started walking, it was getting closer to fall. He was born in the spring. This one evening, we were getting our sorghum pan ready to start cooking sorghum the next day. Suddenly, he started screaming and hollering at the top of his lungs; no one could quiet him. We had other people there as well, part of the crew, but nobody could quiet him, and he didn't give us any clue at that age what the problem was.

Later in the evening, his foot caught someone's attention. It was all black and blue and double in size. My dad held it close to the light and thought he saw tooth marks on his foot. My parents doctored it with home remedies and got him comfortable for the night.

The next morning, they took him to the doctor, while others pitched in and got the sorghum cooking started. The doctor said he got bit by a copperhead snake. Not too much that could be done except to keep him off his foot as much as possible and let it heal. That was a real scare for everyone! We had a lot of copperhead snakes in our area, but seldom did I hear of anyone getting bit.

I really don't remember playing with my brother. I do remember he got tormented a lot and teased to no end. He got called "caterpillar" all the time. He was an angry child, cried a lot, and had a lot of temper tantrums. As I'm writing this, my heart is full of grief and sadness, wondering why I didn't know how or even tried to protect my little brother. It seems to go back to the fact that I didn't believe we deserved any better. The more unhappy we were, the more we fought, the more normal it seemed. What a sick way of thinking!

Yes, that was me, doing this already at a very young age as far back as I can remember. My mom had it in for my brother worse and worse as he got a bit older. She demanded that he be there for her every beck and call. She mentally and emotionally abused him in every way she could. He got more and more sullen and rebellious and would try to run away from her every chance he had. My heart would break for him. It seemed like she thought he had to do for her what no one else had done or could do for her in her own serious unhappiness, and she threw it all on him.

Where my dad was in all this, I don't even know. It seems like he hardened his heart and just turned his ear the other way. Had I known then what caused my mom to be so ugly, so mean, so controlling, so abusive, it could have saved us all a lot of heartache and so much grief later in our lives. This is why I'm writing my story—*my story*—because if I can help one person, just one person (but I plan and pray thousands rather), to avoid the ugliness, the negativity, the heartache, that nobody has to go through this.

God did not intend for anyone to feel so isolated, feel like a victim. He had Jesus die on the cross for you and me so we can be *victors* in Jesus Christ! Church and Christianity should be for us to learn how loving a family is, to learn how much we are loved in Jesus Christ. I will say from my heart that I can well identify and understand why people want to blame God and church for their bitterness. I was definitely one of those people.

I will continue to focus on a bit deeper in my home life growing up. I was eleven years old when our family got blessed with twins—a boy and girl. This is where I stepped in to help with the babies, to bathe them, dress them, play with them, etc. And this is where I had my second compliment from my mom. She told me how much she appreciated me helping with the babies and that I was such a wonderful helper. I loved that little bit of praise so much that I wanted to hear that more often from her.

But she in turn used that bit of compliment to abuse me in every way possible, to guilt me, shame me, which drove me to help more and more in order to hopefully please her. It didn't work that way. It all backfired on me. I was now expected to take over her responsibilities, do her cooking, all the things she always did, basically forcing me to be the parent. She insisted that since she had so little schooling, it is now my job to read cookbooks; to make the food like bread, cakes, etc.

I will say that I learned to enjoy work, probably too much. I felt very duty bound. I did not shirk my duty at all. I could be counted on to take responsibility for whatever I was asked to do. But this, in turn, also turned me into a workhorse slave. I tried to get my siblings to pitch in, which they probably did to a certain extent, but because I somehow became the slave, I could not get my parents, either one, to help support me in that they all needed to help pitch in and make the load lighter for everyone. They would both get angry at me and not listen to anything I said. So I carried more and more bitterness around and worked harder to try and appease and make peace, but that was all to no avail.

I realize now that the bottom line of everything was no one was willing to take any responsibility for any actions. I learned how to be the best liar and didn't wince about it because if I said I did something wrong or whatever it was, I got punished to no end with heaps of guilt and shame and condemnation poured heavily all over me.

That, in itself, drove me to hate myself more and more. How ugly I am, how totally worthless I am because is all I deserve. It boiled down to one thing in my mind: my mom is as ugly as she can be at home, and if we heard someone knocking on the door, she changed instantly to this beautiful smiling face, glowing in happiness and as cheerful as could be. She would communicate with the people, smile and carry on, the whole house turned from chaos to instant sweetness in the blink of an eye.

This totally would blow my mind every time. I would watch my mom, and wonder, how or why does she treat us so terribly, but she suddenly treats the other people in our midst like saints? In my mind I would try to picture that a person could just always focus on being kind, not be so two-faced.

I had written earlier how I was born screaming with earache. My ear problems continued, having so many ear infections that I became basically deaf. I could hear very little in my young years. I learned how to read lips so I could figure out what people were saying. I believe now that is how I learned so much in body language. That is what I focused on to cope, to hear was watch body language. I was a loner in turn because of it. I internalized everything.

I also see now that because of my hearing impairment, it caused me to think deeper, and I had to concentrate so hard in what people were saying directly to me.

I always focused more on their facial expressions than what someone was actually saying to me. For me, my ears sounded like a freight truck as loud as could be was always roaring in my head. This is all I knew. I believe sometimes that I could have heard better, but it was my way of blocking everything out. That was easy for me to do, and that was one of my ways I learned and used as a tool to cope.

We had a store in our house and also outside. The groceries were right in our kitchen! A corner of it was full of shelves with all the grocery items. The large pantry, which was probably a bedroom at one time, was held with all the bulk items. People could roam freely through part of the kitchen, living room on into the pantry. The living room and kitchen were long and more narrow, so both served as part store.

The living room was used to host the salesmen who came to get our store orders. My dad had a nice little table for that. The grocery trucks were unloaded in the living room. There was no space to store anything, so as young as I can remember, it was us children's job to help carry everything away. We stored boxes of groceries in our bedrooms upstairs!

The house was two houses built together to make one roomy house for a large family, which served very well for us. We had two staircases, two bedrooms in each one, and a large bedroom downstairs where my parents slept and kept the babies till they were around three then got moved upstairs The one was used for us girls to sleep in, and the other one was packed full with all the groceries.

When we got company overnight, us girls had to give up one bedroom for our guests. I was sleeping in that room, and I ended up sleeping on the couch a lot. My bedroom was the only one with a door. The other room had only curtains. Somehow, the young sisters ended up sleeping with me. That made me become very responsible to where I felt the need to fill in the gap to be a parent, which was not healthy at all. I wasn't just the big sister, I was "the parent" filling in the empty gap that my mom did not want to be responsible for.

To this day, my sisters are still holding that against me in a deep grudge. I pray and trust that someday, they can make peace with themselves about it. The subject is an extremely touchy one because all the good that I thought I was responsible for or helped grow together in the family all came crashing down later in our family, which caused the worst nightmare a family could ever have in their lives, not because of what I've done but because of what happened in a family that had put everything on an artificial facade. More on that subject later.

CHAPTER 4

WEIGHT

I always had a lot of weight problems as long as I remember. I was mocked, poked fun at, jabbing fingers into my belly as my stomach was always big. And this included my older cousins. It made me feel very inferior. I ate a lot to satisfy something. Sweets were my big go-to. It made me crawl into a shell.

I was never nice. People didn't even want me to wait on them in the store; they would tell my sister to wait on them because I was too mean and grouchy. That isolated me even more. I didn't know that all I needed was someone to speak positive words into me.

My teachers tried. They mostly were very critical. I was constantly getting in trouble about something, and the teacher had no problem whipping me and sending a note home for my dad, then he whipped me again. I personally didn't ever know what I was doing wrong. It was also confirmed to me that this is all I deserve because I couldn't hear, and so I must have appeared very rebellious and stubborn.

Of course that just added the bitterness and anger to the already heavy load I was carrying. I started doing these crazy fasting diets when I was a young teenager. I was so determined to lose weight. I went on this ten-day or two-week fasting with no food, only apple juice. I had less and less energy as the days went by. I got mocked and jeered for what I was doing, but I was determined to stick it out and I did.

Of course, I was feeling so bad about myself, so what did I do? Yes, you guessed it: gouged on sweets, baked goods—whatever we had around till I was stuffed. I remember how horrible that made me feel. For the most part, I didn't keep eating once I felt full, which is probably what saved me from a life of too much chaos.

One thing I am very grateful for and will always thank my parents for, we always had very consistent meals. Breakfast was a nutritious meal with eggs from our farm. And homemade cheese that we made and ate a lot but sold many, many round delicious cheeses that I spent many hours helping my mom make on our trusty old wood stove in the winter and in the summer, we had a woodstove on our back porch that was used for cooking all our meals and for canning and cheese making.

We usually had four cows my oldest sister and my dad milked and always had thirty or more cheeses curing on our many shelves in various places in our house that I was responsible to help care for, turning the cheeses every morning and evening and rubbing a bit of oil on them to keep them from getting moldy or too dry. We used white cheesecloths that we made out of old sheets. Mom would hem them so they didn't get threads into the cheese. My job was to care for the other animals. I never milked. Finally at age twenty, I taught myself how to milk a cow! That required a lot of determination because my fingers and hands got so sore!

Because of my miserable state of mind, the older I got, the meaner I got! I was twelve when a tragedy happened in school. I knew how to cause drama in school. By now, everyone would come and ask me what is wrong with me. My anger just escalated, and I had no problem in venting whatever way I could. I was supposed to be the itter in playing a game of free tag. I don't remember what the problem was, but in looking back, I was probably angry and yelling at everyone, insisting I didn't get caught.

So here I was with having no choice. I closed my eyes, counted to the usual number out loud, and shouting that I'm now coming to find everyone. If the players ran to the base before the itter, they would yell, "Free!"

and could go hide again. And the person who didn't get to the base first was caught and then was now *it*.

It was very muddy out. The snow had thawed—a February day, nice out to play. Our base was a big tree sitting on a bank with the driveway on the bottom and a bank on top, so we could run from any direction, and the itter sometimes couldn't see too well. I'm looking around for any faces peeping out of hiding places.

Suddenly, I see my two boy cousins come running full speed from the bank part of the tree. I'm below the tree on the muddy driveway. I ran to the tree, yelling their names, and the next thing I know, I'm lying twenty feet or more away from the base and screaming at the top of my lungs that my leg is broken. Everyone is now looking out of their hiding places, shouting at me to be quiet and that there is nothing wrong with me. Since I had just caused an ugly scene a few minutes prior, they believed I was having another temper tantrum.

But I didn't listen. I kept up my screams, so everyone slowly came to look and were horrified to discover that indeed my leg was broken. The biggest bone right above my ankle was broken clean off on my left leg. The teacher suddenly took action. Everyone had to grab their coats for me to lie on, as I wouldn't let anyone touch me. I was hysterical with the pain.

The boys ran for help. There were no phones. My dad was helping our neighbors pack up to move. He was there in short order with a kind gentleman bringing him with his truck. No one could touch me, so they found an old door to roll me on and slid me in the truck somehow, and to the hospital emergency room we went.

What a subdued bunch of children all stood around watching. This mean, ugly monster just got hurt! There was nothing to say. I never have heard the story of what happened. I only recall that one boy got a broken nose and broken glasses; the other one had a broken toe or two from the mishap. From what I can recall now, they must have slid down the bank like ice and hit me and sent me flying in the air. I had no relationship with any of them because of my ugly attitude, so I never asked, and nobody ever talked to me about it.

I was in the hospital overnight, and then my aunt took me to her home for several weeks to care for me. I had to learn how to use crutches. My leg was in a heavy white cast all the way up to my hip. I ended up having a cast on my leg for six months. Two of those months were in a walking cast.

For years, I struggled with my leg. It was never set properly, and because it was cast for so long, my broken leg was shorter. I limped for years. It also caused me a lot of hip problems. After years of working with chiropractors and change of diet, my leg is finally all healed up and no more numbness where the break was. My hip is also fine too now.

I believe that mellowed me a lot. I was stuck. Now I had to depend on everyone to help me till I learned how to navigate my crutches and drag my heavy cast around. I never did hear anything about the episode, except casual remarks in passing that no one likes me as I have such horrible attitudes. People were even afraid to come visit me! They probably didn't know if I would lash out at them. The children especially stayed out of my way.

Now that I was stuck in the house with a cast, it became my full responsibility to take care of the twins. They were six months old. They were learning to crawl and everything else.

Mom also took advantage of my disability to the fullest. I was her slave. She pushed all the house responsibilities on me. I had learned from my experience to now shut down even more and bottle everything up and also pretend to be someone that I wasn't. My struggles got more severe.

CHAPTER 5

MY GRANDMOTHER

I don't know my grandmother as a nice person. They lived right beside us in a cute home with Grandfather and my great aunt living there to care for my grandparents. She never married. she cheerfully did all the household duties.

I loved my aunt! I would go there often as a young girl. My sisters and I usually went together.

For some reason, my dear grandmother did not like me. She would find a reason to whip me whenever she could. She had a belt that she suddenly would demand that I bring to her. I would go get it and carry it to her, fearing for my life. Her face would get all ugly and mean. She would grab me and make me lie down in her lap, and she would whip me on and on—I screaming and she whipping. Finally the demons in her would be satisfied, and I would run away from her.

I was seven and eight when she mostly did this, so I made sure I never went over there anymore to stay. Only when my mom sent me for an errand would I go cautiously to my aunt and ask her for what I needed. Grandfather had to obey orders too: catch me and tie me to the porch post. She would run after me to try and catch me. I would scream and run to my mom. Mom would not even tell her to leave me alone. She would catch me and whip me right in front of my mom, then when she was satisfied in hurting me, she would go back home. I was terrified of my grandmother.

Grandmother loved and adored my sister next to me. She worshipped the ground she walked on. She spent a lot of time there, learning her language, and they just enjoyed each other to the fullest. She gave my sister gifts and was always doting and bragging on her.

Of course, that bothered me. I tried my best to be kind and good to her. One day, I decided I'm learning her language and speak it to her since she was so drawn to my sister over that. The day came when I so proudly went to her and started speaking her language with the best that I knew. She looked at me and started mocking and jeering me to no end. She proceeds to tell me that she hates my guts because I am just like my dad and his family. She said she likes my sister best because she is *just like her*. Sticking her finger in my face, she told me

I will never speak her language, and she will never like me.

The word *love* was a foreign word to me. I didn't realize it then, but she had put a curse over me and my life. I found out many years later. God told a preacher that as he was trying to help me through to Christ as I was dealing with my bitter, ugly, ugly heart. In my growing-up years, I would wake up during the night and find an ugly black being by my bed. It always looked like a woman. I never saw this woman looking at me, just standing there, and she would be holding something, which I always thought looked like a clock. Was I scared? It doesn't seem like I was. I would lie there and stare till this thing would finally be gone.

My mom always said that grandmother had a nervous breakdown of some sort when she was young, and it made her crazy. Many times at night, Grandfather would come banging on our window to wake up Dad and Mom to come over and help because Grandmother is having hysteric fits. They would later tell us what they were doing during the night.

Somehow, I got involved as well. One night, Grandfather came over, and it happened that our parents woke my sister and me up to go so sit over there as well. I could hear her screams from our house as I ran on the path from our house to theirs. I recall us all going in her room to try and calm her down, but nobody could wake her up. She just continued on and on. We finally went home because there was nothing anyone could do.

The next day, she didn't wake up till noon. I and others were there, waiting to see if she says anything. We were not allowed to say anything about the episode but were to see if she talks about it. Her eyes were all bloodshot, and she was very quiet, and conversing with her was basically impossible. I was very concerned for my grandmother and wanted to show it, but it was otherwise a hopeless case. I still made sure I stayed away from her so she can't hurt me.

CHAPTER 6

CHURCH

I was born and raised in a plain setting with no running water, no phones, no electric, no motors. It was our life, our culture in the Old Order Mennonite setting. I'm glad I got to live that way. I'm grateful that I had the privilege to learn many good principals with living life to the fullest with family and friends and get to go to church and learn about God.

I took God very seriously. I really believed that reading my Bible and going to church and praying were very important. It left me very confused with the way we lived at home and my mom going to church acting like the sweetest saint there ever was.

Our church setting was a bit unusual, but I loved it, and it was small. The congregation had been much bigger, but many people dropped out and joined other places as they were obviously not very committed to living this way. To them, it was obviously just a lifestyle, and they didn't see any need for that, so they left and joined other more modern churches or moved away to something that better suited their preference.

The church had been a new adventure that two preachers started in the 1940s. So many, many people came together from walks of life all over to attend this church and grow together as a community because they had a mission, a strong mission that drew many people. That mission was to go simpler and plainer, not follow the ways of the world.

My parents had joined their parents to all go start a new community in a different state as the community outgrew the church house quickly. Dad and Mom were not married; they simply came with their parents, and of course, something drew them together after a while, and they wedded in a sweet, romantic way. Mom would share how they had fifty dollars to their name. They lived with both sets of parents. I was born at one home; my oldest sister was born at the other home! Shortly after I was born, my parents bought the farm with a house and barn ready to move in. This is where I grew up until we moved away when I was seventeen years old to a different state, where the community was now all trying to move to one setting.

The large family had just decided to move back to their homeland to be with family members. They found out the father had cancer. And that same year, my dad also set up the store! It is still running today, and it has grown tremendously and attracts people from all over. People always loved spending time in the general store part. This was totally separate from the house and a cute old building with no heat in it even that I recall! We would just freeze out there.

My dad found beautiful pieces of anything you can imagine to sell in there: a lot of cedar items, little chests, etc. I still have a little cedar chest of drawers that stands four inches tall and two inches wide with two drawers. I cherish it as I know it was handpicked by my dad, and he always proudly showed off his wares! Many sturdy stainless steel cookware got sold along with supplies for horses, saddles, harnesses, horseshoes of any shape and size you can imagine, dishes (unusual dishes, not just regular glassware), melamine dishes that lasted forever! I still have all mine and use them daily! That is my favorite plate to eat out of. Stainless steel cookie sheets and cake pans that will never wear out, unless you drive over them! They will stay in the family as wonderful, useful heirlooms forever, not just sitting on a shelf, being afraid to use them for fear they will break. I treasure each piece I have gotten, handed down from my grandparents and even given as gifts from the teachers when going to school. And yes, the memory still remains which teacher gave what!

Our church and school were always in the same building. We didn't have an actual church house; it was in an old house that nobody lived in. Down a steep hill, we lived in a beautiful setting with lots of woods, hills, mountains, and very rural. My dad's brother was the ordained preacher.

My uncle got deathly ill when I was very young. He battled cancer for at least six years. My aunt took care of him so faithfully, and they traveled a lot out of state to do doctoring. It was devastating when my dear uncle got worse and his cancer spread from his colon to his brain. He died very shortly after that. I *was* eleven years old when he passed. They had seven living children. Two children had died as infants. Their children were older, and the youngest was my age. They were still all living at home and had faithfully taken over the farm duties for many years prior. This was how they made their income.

Raising cane and making sorghum were the community's biggest means of support. People came from all over to watch us cook sorghum molasses, all done by horses and horsepower. Picture taking was frowned on, but I recall my dad always telling people that when they ask, we say no, but if they do it without asking, we just don't say anything.

We got very popular when someone took pictures and had them put in *National Geographic* magazine! We started getting letters from all over the world! My dad seemed really happy about that even if he didn't approve of picture taking. I have one picture of when I was a little girl, so all my pictures are just vivid memories in my mind.

I recall the very last sermon my uncle preached. Little did any of us realize it would be his last one. He preached about dying, and he preached to the young people, begging them to turn to God, as we had rebellious youngsters in our congregation. He then recited the song,

> On Jordan's stormy banks I stand
> And cast a wishful eye
> To Canaan's fair and happy land
> Where my Possessions lie.

I don't recall if he recited the whole song, but I know he did the first verse.

Shortly after my uncle passed away, our lives took a turn for so much sadness and loneliness. The family decided to move away to the bigger community where they would have more church people to interact with and young people to socialize with. By now, our church had only a few remaining families. My mom's sister-in-law and her three children attended. Her husband did not attend. He left the church at a very young age and married a woman from what we call "society status," then brought her back to the community. She joined the church. My mom's sister brought all her children, but her husband didn't attend anymore. He was excommunicated from the church as long as I can recall. My mom's first cousin and his two girls attended.

The older girl cousins did have a huge impact on me. On Sundays, we would sing together and learn new songs. We usually ate together at church, then after lunch, we youngsters got together in a circle and would sing our hearts out. Our songbooks consisted of church and Sunday school hymnals and ninety-eight selected songs then various German songbooks as well. The girls had friends outside of the church that taught them many new songs. They would spend all afternoon singing and teaching us new songs.

I loved singing! I memorized nearly all the songs in the ninety-eight selected songbooks. My dad always requested the same song to be sung: "Will the circle be unbroken? By and by, by and by." And his favorite song in the other book was "There Were Ninety and Nine that Safely Lay."

My mom had an unusual musical singing voice. I loved singing, but I got mocked to no end about my singing. But I kept right on singing anyways! Now that my uncle has passed, the sad changes, who will be the preacher? The big church preachers came in. The decision was made since the congregation is so small, with my uncle's family moving, that my dad would be the speaker, and preachers would take turns to come help us have church. I believe someone came once a month. Now we had many visitors in our home. We had to hire young men as well to come help cook sorghum, young girls to come teach school.

There were now always people in our home. It didn't seem to affect us. My dad loved to be hospitable; my mom, not so much. In looking back, I don't recall her ever complain about all the visitors, workers in our home—sometimes up to five people. I recall all the good times we had! Sunday afternoons, all us young people would gather together and pile up on a big two-horse wagon with hay bales for our seats, and away we drove, singing, laughing, talking, and enjoying the scenery as we went to explore caves and cliffs, running down steep hills, grabbing whatever we could so we don't roll down the hill—and panting, barely able to crawl up the hills! Yes, those are pleasant memories.

With the church having had so many people leaving, and some of them even claimed to be atheists, the ban was very strictly applied, and many hearts got broken and/or crushed. I learned very young to judge people, to think that everyone is going to hell who is now banned or not part of our church.

The day my grandmother bought her gas refrigerator was a traumatic day for me. My dad sat us down and told us that she is going to hell because she bought the refrigerator and is very disobedient to God. That scared me, but I believed every word my dad said. My mom must not have cared, or maybe she just wasn't going to listen or both. I recall my mom giving me a plastic cup and telling me to go over there and ask my aunt for a cup of cream. I timidly went over there, knowing what my dad had said and now very confused how we would want any part of the forbidden fruit, but yet not defying what my mom requested.

I was eleven years old when my uncle and aunt got put in the ban. They had eight children, seven boys and one girl. One son was my age, so we went to school together till then. My dad and I had traveled to the original church before the whole congregation moved away and settled elsewhere. He took me to a good ear doctor there who put tubes in my ears, and I actually regained fifty percent of my hearing back.

After church the bishop made an announcement that they have a ban letter to read and officialize. The letter stated that my uncle did not listen to put away his chainsaw, so the ban is now on them. They are now cutting off their connection with God. I was devastated and so confused.

Our church is now much smaller. We had church in their old house. Now the church was in homes, taking turns. School had to be moved—such a sad time. We were not allowed to interact with their children. We had to treat them like outcasts. The pain everyone carried was devastating for me. It didn't seem like anyone in the church cared. The suffering in silence continued for me. The rejection I was taught—give the cold shoulder—was very damaging for me. It was like a deep, dark cloud hung everywhere, and yet life had to continue.

CHAPTER 7

DARKNESS

THE NIGHT'S SO DARK.
IT'S THE ONLY WAY TO DO IT.
SHOVE EVERYTHING UNDER THE RUG AND
NEVER LOOK AT WHAT IS HIDING.

This chapter is a part that I don't want to write, but I know in my heart that the only way to make this book of my life more complete is for this to be included. At a very young age, I struggled with purity. I wanted to pretend I was a boy. I never felt feminine that I can recall. I was always told and mocked that I have big hands like a man. My shoulders are not like a woman's; they represent a man. My body has no curves. I look like a man from the back.

Since my parents carried a deep, dark secret about a moral tragedy that happened to my mom at a very young age, with her resulting to having a baby through incest at fourteen years of age—a little girl that was not normal. She died at the young tender age of three years old. My dear mother was totally innocent and, at that age, did not even know where babies came from or what caused babies to be and being born. Everything was a hush-hush situation.

My grandmother treated her daughter so badly, berating and degrading her in every way to where her mind just totally shut down, and she never allowed herself to even think of how beautiful and normal she really is. The only thing she knew was to push everyone out of her life and put a huge wall up, so she knew nothing, saw nothing, only survival.

When my parents were getting ready to marry, the decision was somehow made that this must stay hidden. It will never be discussed. If children are born, nobody will ever know. How my dad even found out about it is something I cannot answer.

My mom and her family also moved to this community, like many, many others that came and went. This community was not an established church, so many denominations of every sort, we can only imagine, made their way into this culture, looking for a church that would satisfy their hunger, their need for a Savior, thinking that *church* could/would give them what they so desperately needed, and wanting man/ church to fix them and all their problems, which resulted in a lot of very bad immoral pasts that no one knew how to deal with or help people become clean and undefiled. This then filtered into the church with the children carrying the generational curse that was supposed to be so well hidden and never talked about, with plans and determination that the less you teach your children, the more innocent they are, and nothing bad could or would ever happen in this great church setting.

Seemingly, each family and individual carried a lot of garbage with them, and the church became infested with a huge epidemic that was supposed to remain hush-hush in hopes that it will all just disappear on its own. Also that the church must represent its perfection to the fullest to look good to the appearance and hiding everything with works, the struggles and ugliness have to be carried as part of our struggles with being a Christian. Bad behaviors were acted out because of all the unresolved issues, but this was all excused away for whatever excuse and reason. Teaching everyone to be more deceptive and learning how to hide everything under cover and be a two-faced person more than ever, living a life of pain and hurt inside but covering it all up with trying to please people in every way possible, which was readily accepted. This was who we were looked at, and nothing else was supposed to come out of us. These were learned behaviors that were taught in our setting. It was all they knew. In their thinking, they really believed this is what the Bible teaches.

Here I am, struggling with moral issues as long as I can remember. My cousins violated me in many ways. Molestation was at an all high. In looking back, it almost seemed like we were just like animals; boys had absolutely no healthy respect for girls and me.

I didn't know better. I didn't know to run. I thought, *Finally, someone likes me.* What a terrible thinking! With all the dirty immorality going on, God must have really had his hand over me at a very young age. I had made up my mind that no boy is going to touch me, no matter what, before I was twelve years old. In looking back, I realize this saved me from a horrible life of regrets and ugliness.

When I was eleven I was rocking my baby sister. Suddenly, this deep longing came over me, so real, so heart rendering. I started praying deep from my heart, tears pouring down my face, *God, I want to be a Christian. I want to get to know the* real you. *Show me how to get that.*

I realize that God heard me then and there. How did I know that my family and church people didn't really believe in the *real, true God?* I didn't, but something deep inside of me ignited and has carried me into the next bitter years of my life. I had made that resolution in my heart about being a good, moral girl even though I was molested a lot when I was young, but I didn't allow that to define who I was. I had no idea how these things would affect me in later life nor how it would draw the wrong people/person into my life when the time came to date.

I will add here that all the things I wrote are things that I've processed over the years, and also what I wrote about my mom, I finally found out when I was twenty years old. My parents did not tell me. My first reaction was, if only I had known all this sooner, it would have spared me so much grief and ugliness, and I would have understood better why my mom is so very mean. I don't recall ever talking to any of my family members about all this corruption going on in our church. I was just a loner. There was very little I talked to with anyone. It seems like I was too busy being miserable and just trying to cope. I will move on to another phase of this story to make everything come together better.

CHAPTER 8

MY DAD AND I

I definitely need to write about my dad in a deeper way too. My dad had a lot of influence in my life, and his deep, good influence he had on me helped me way later in life that I now better understand as I've continued to grow more in grace and peace toward my own self. Dad was a very loving person. He had a warm influence about him that has stuck with me always till now. He would have us girls sit around him many an evening and tell us Bible stories, making them so vivid that those Bible stories have never left me. This was when I was very young.

He did not continue this when the other children started coming along. He did read Bible every morning, and we always knelt together, and he prayed out loud. One touching thing, he always said grace at the table too before meals and after we were done. He was so used to praying that when he got dementia, nothing stopped him from saying his prayers, even though he was not aware of any of his surroundings. That would always bring tears to my eyes, knowing how devoted he was.

I believe in my heart that my mom's negative behaviors played a huge impact on him, so subtle that he didn't realize who he was becoming. Our daily routine and schedule are what kept the family from going under. But having a loving, warm family relationship together got lost very early on in my life, which is probably why I felt so insecure, unhappy, and plain miserable. Our mealtimes were no longer pleasant; it was bickering, and Mom constantly belittling someone at the table or nagging dad about something that he didn't do right.

Dad spent very little time in the house. He was always helping his mom or in the shop/store and very busy on the farm, plowing, whatever needed done. I still marvel at how much my dad got done in a day. He had to go far to farm, and he never complained about it being too hard. He was always faithful in being home for meals. Our store also brought in many out-of-state people to come buy our unusual goods that my dad carried. Many times, he would come in to ask or tell Mom to make extra food and set more plates on the table. "We are having guests!" That was always exciting! I know we never served any fancy meals, and no, we never ate at a restaurant either. I didn't know what that word even meant!

I was always fascinated at my dad's stories. He had a great memory and knew exactly what year everything happened. I would hear him fondly relating how the church started, with them coming on the scene driving a car and at eight years old. The new life of horse and buggy began. People loved spending time with my dad, and that is what I observed. I never heard my dad say a bad word. He would reach out to the needy people who came to our store. People could have their groceries on credit. Each regular customer had their own little sales book. My dad would give them so many days of grace period, then he would somehow navigate with the customers about payment. The poor people, he always gave them more grace and let them get more groceries.

It didn't matter what the situation was, Dad did not get us involved in the finances. That was his own load he carried, and I know God blessed him greatly for his loving-kindness, as I know and observed that he always did it as a ministry and not as a punishment on anyone. That in itself made a huge impact on me and helped shape and form me to who I am today.

He always had time for people. Since our community was so small, and after my uncle died, my dad was the only man member in the church. He loved to serve. He loved to minister. My mom never said anything good or bad about it, but in looking back, I realize she did not support him either. She played the role of a good sport while in the process, but I especially always had to suffer for it later. She didn't hesitate to find someone to abuse when no visitors or customers were around.

I loved spending time with my dad every chance I had. I was the little tomboy! It didn't bother me to get dirty, whatever I had to do to try and spend as much time as I could. He would also make it clear that when we spent time with him, we were not allowed to talk much. He wanted to use that time to think. And now I realize that was a very good thing. I learned to enjoy the quietness and peace. That is probably why my dad was so very productive.

He wore a lot of hats, and he wore them well in my eyes, except when he was around Mom, then he was different, like he closed his mind off completely around her. He never shamed her in front of us children. I never heard him correct her, criticize her, or anything of that sort. He always demanded that we respect her and listen to her, which is probably why Daddy whipped us when she told him to, to show his support.

Dad didn't believe in having fun. I don't recall him ever playing with us children. The older we got, the more critical he got with everything we did. That definitely stemmed from the very bad negativity in the home. That caused me a lot of confusion. He was always stable and kind when I spent time with him alone.

The time had come for my parents to make a very weighty decision. We would have to move, to the bigger community where everyone had now settled. It was three hours from where we lived. A place came available that had a very old house and barn on it. We would have to build a new house and a store, as no buildings were available for us to use as a store.

Our uncle and aunt had a store until we come to take that position. They lived just right across from where we bought this property. We had over one hundred acres where we lived now, and this property only had around forty acres. Dad was very concerned about that as we children were growing bigger and older, and downsizing like that would result in a huge problem with making enough income to provide for the family. He did not want to move. I didn't really understand it then, but I do now. He knew he couldn't be the man he was here where he enjoyed living. His ministry would have to end, his rights to be a decision maker would be ripped out from under him, thus causing our family to fall down a terrible landslide.

I'm sure he had no idea what ugliness would result from moving, but what else was he going to do? The church had strict rules a member had to abide by, and if they saw what they call rebellion and disobedience, then the serious punishment was applied. My dad knew that and nobody wanted to have that label nor to be excommunicated and shunned. Now also be rejected and judged that a person is now headed straight to hell, my dad would not tolerate such a thing, so he dragged his feet. And he dragged his feet. Reliving that episode now as I'm writing it and trying to picture my dad putting his thoughts into something really helps me understand why the next phase of our life turned into a destruction.

CHAPTER 9

THE BIG MOVE

REBUILDING IS ALWAYS A CHOICE.

I was seventeen when we moved to this strange, scary, big community. My youngest sister was eighteen months old. Now there were ten of us children, eight girls and two boys. Everything suddenly changed in our lives. We were used to living in a small community; we did everything together, all the families connected. There was no separation of age, gender, etc. Suddenly, we are expected to interact with strictly these young people. We were now expected to join this clique that I seriously detested, but lo and behold, I learned quickly to be the very religious person that we had been trained to become. I am now one of them, knowing exactly how to play my part, and I did it very passionately and seriously.

My parents were not happy that they had to move. Mom became sullen, very bitter, angry, and hostile. Now when people came over, instead of playing her part like she always did before, she now was no longer sociable. She would ignore everyone, her head hanging low, sitting there with her eyes closed, completely blocking life and people out. I would be so humiliated and embarrassed at how my mom was acting. People would ask me what is wrong with my mom. I didn't know. I did not ever connect any of this, but in my later years, I have tried to process all of this, and now it is all unfolding in my mind as I'm writing my story. It is giving me so much freedom, knowing that the answers are flowing so beautiful together yet so tragic.

My dad, the man I looked up to always, knowing he had his flaws—and I accepted his flaws with grace—he alarmed me greatly. I recall that I was so filled with fear and confusion about my dear dad that I actually started writing journal and learned how to process my feelings. I have been writing journal ever since then, not on a continual basis but on and off over the years.

Dad started having the worst temper tantrums. I recall the very first episode; he is yelling and carrying on about something that one of his children did that he didn't like. I went up to him, asking him about his behavior in a kind manner as I was so shocked. He yelled back at me that he can act however he wants to, but we are not allowed to act that way. His response nearly knocked me over. I became numb with confusion. I still tried to spend time with my dad.

I finally mustered up enough courage to ask him why Mom is so mean. He told me long ago he gave up on Mom, but he expects us children to honor and respect her. That helped me to continue trying to be the daughter I need to be. I tried so hard to please my mom. It did not make any difference. The family was now nothing but a forced setting. I learned to dull my feelings by laughing. I soon had all the girls laughing at the table. We spent hours giggling over nothing. It helped me cope with life, but later in life, it bit me hard, where I had to learn I couldn't laugh.

The younger children suffered the most. My parents no longer wanted the responsibility of raising the children. Now we older ones were supposed to lead the way. That didn't work either, as they saw that slipping out of work was easy: tattle to daddy, and he would tell us older ones to leave the younger ones alone. Wow! Now we had a real problem! Of course, we had all learned to be this perfect family in church and if people were around, so it was never obvious.

I recall sharing my heart with my first cousin how bad things were at home. They were a happy family. She went to her siblings about it. Next thing I know, one of their family members comes to tell mom what I said.

Now my life turns completely upside down. Mom never stopped with her punishments on me. My hatred toward her just got deeper and uglier.

Since we had many people of all backgrounds come to visit the church which was growing rapidly, and also move there. There was a family living there long before we moved there that had five children. The boys were older, and the girls were born in the community. They were a family that drove a vehicle when they came, and they then sold their vehicle and decided to make that their home church.

Personally, they didn't intrigue me too much. They were just a family living in the community. Two of the boys, the oldest ones, got baptized when I did. I was almost nineteen when I joined the church. I was looked down on for not doing it younger, but I wanted to make sure I was ready. I wanted to be saved, and I knew I wasn't. I finally prayed to God and felt some change over me, but I knew something drastically was missing. I did not feel any love in my heart, nor did I know how to forgive my mom, and that really bothered me. I convinced myself with all the sermons I heard that this is just how it is. These are struggles that God is talking about that we will have. I prayed a lot. I read my Bible. I took this Christian life very serious, but I knew I had no peace.

We had the store. We got it moved over to our new store building. Everything was in one building. No more store in the house! It was so different to have large community of like-minded people now coming to shop. I loved taking care of the store. I was my dad's right-hand helper. Young boys liked to come in and visit with us girls. Now that we had the store all in one building, it was easy for us to be in there visiting.

Somehow in the process, this young man started coming to the store a lot when he figured out the times I was in there. I had no idea that he had something in mind beside just liking to talk. Since we had been used to visitors all the time in our small home church, to me, talking to a boy was nothing unusual. I had high goals for myself. To me, it was important that a young man will be someone that I like and respect for me to date him. In this church, it was a known thing: you marry the young man you date.

I was horrified when I was approached by my boy cousins, telling me that this young man likes me. I saw nothing that attracted me to him. I don't recall what I told my cousins, but I do remember them spending a lot of time convincing me that I need to like this young man. One day, he finally asked me for a date. I was taken aback. I told him that he needs to ask my dad if he can date me. I thought it was a good way to get rid of him, but he did exactly that! I didn't know what to think.

My dad had made a rule that none of us are allowed to accept a young man asking us out until we were twenty. I was relieved. Great! Now I can tell him that, and he will leave. I wrote my letter, writing what my dad said to write. He was very distraught that this young man asked me; he didn't seem to like him very well. My dad was hoping he would forget about me, and so did I.

Several people found out about it, and everyone told me I need to give him a chance. I didn't really understand why I should and made my case clear. I was told that I should feel sorry for him, as his parents had left over some squabble and ditched the older boys. They had to fend for themselves, and they each moved in with a family.

I started hearing disturbing stories about this young man. I was in a turmoil. Now people want me to feel sorry for him? I really didn't understand that at all. He was four years older, and people thought he really needed a wife and I would be that perfect person for him.

I still wasn't convinced. I was going to let my dad make that decision should he decide to ask me again once I turned twenty. I was not going to undermine my dad. I really did respect and honor him for being my dad, even though he was no longer the same man I grew up with. He had now lost all his ability to be the father of the home. He no longer even looked at it that he should or could be the decision maker in the home. It was like he chose to be a victim now, rather he became our conscience and allowed the church to make all his decisions. I believe he got mentally beat down so much by the church because they were taking all his rights away.

I wanted my dad to help me make the decision, nobody else. Instead, he went to the bishop, the main decision maker of the church. Everything had to be run by to him. He was the one who baptized everyone. He married all the couples. He was the "all authority" in the church. This young man had lived with them for a while before he moved to his own little place that he bought land and built a harness shop that he lived in half of it. He had learned the art of saddle and harness making and everything else that goes with it—bridles, halters, etc.

From the not-so-good things I was hearing, I believed in my heart that the bishop would give dad some good solid advice. He told my dad I need to give him a chance. My dad came home heavyhearted. He shared that he was not happy. He didn't believe in this young man, but now he doesn't feel that he has a choice; we must do what the bishop said.

I wrote him my letter of approval. He was ecstatic. I was very skeptical but learned to see the good in him. He was a very friendly, outgoing young man, and with our background of being with all kinds of people, I never realized his agenda behind this whole thing. Somehow, he had learned about all that had transpired in the immorality. My younger sisters had no problem sharing with him everything they knew. I personally didn't know what they knew but found out later their lives were just as marred as mine.

I was totally innocent in all this horrible situation. I believed in keeping myself pure. I enjoyed spending time with him, and he spent a lot of time at our house, which I thought was probably all good since my parents were around; it seemed like a good supervised situation. He became the family best friend, always there for the younger children, doing everything, and they were smitten. They loved his attention. I was still leary, but all looked well and seemed well.

Little did I know the tragedy that was about to unfold. He wanted help with his shop. He asked my dad if two girls could come; that way, one is not alone. My dad gladly obliged. We were getting ready for our wedding. I was now twenty-one. He wanted to marry me at twenty. My dad said a flat no! That caused some major issues. We had already dated for almost a year. He said he will not let us marry till I'm almost twenty-two. He kept dragging his feet. He was not happy whom my oldest sister had married; that made him give more strict rules because he kept saying he can't let his girls marry off so fast.

We got married. I was a happy bride. My life was full and sweet. My husband treated me wonderfully, or so

I thought. My brothers and sisters were at our house *a lot*. I thought this was so great. Everyone seemed happy. We all had great times together.

Baby number one was born. How exciting! I loved being a mom. A little girl. My heart was full. Trouble started arising: complaints, problems, bickering, people coming over to lecture my husband. Accusations were thrown at him that he is committing immorality. Things just kept getting worse. I was getting worn to frazzles. Chaos after chaos from church people. I'm thinking, *You told me to marry him. I trusted your judgment completely. Now this?*

I had gotten deathly ill with infection in my blood when baby girl was two weeks old. I had to quit breast-feeding my precious baby. When our second little girl came along, the older had just turned one year old. This sweet little girl had to get rushed to the hospital at eight days old. She had a blocked aorta and many other heart problems. I was shocked and horrified when the preachers caused a great disturbance and said to the doctor that surgery is not necessary; she can just die. The other preacher was kinder. He told the doctor to go ahead and do surgery.

We had no rights to make any decisions for our beautiful baby girl. Because we did what was right and best, the church said they will not help pay the hospital bill or anything. They insisted that we went against all their church rules. We had the midwife at our house, and she told us to rush her to the doctor. When a baby is dying right in front of your eyes and you don't know what's wrong with her, why wouldn't we do what the doctor says?

Tragedy after tragedy happened. My husband got excommunicated shortly after this ordeal happened. More chaos. More drama. More what? Two more children were born, all in three years. Now we had three girls and one boy.

The story got out when my sister ran away from home. She told someone what had been going on before we were ever even married. I was shocked and horrified. Two of my cousins came over to tell me. My husband was not at home. They went to the neighbors and borrowed a gun, planning to wait around so they could shoot him when he arrives home. I saw them sneaking around out there, going from tree to tree. I opened up the door and asked them what they are doing and told them to leave. They turned their deaf ears on me. I got scared, really scared. The babies were in bed, I was walking around, frantic, wishing there was a way I could make them leave.

Suddenly, I hear the gunshot go off. It felt like the whole house exploded. I panicked. I didn't know what nor whom they shot. I went into total shock. When my husband came home, then I knew they didn't kill him. Instead, they had dragged our beautiful, sweet, loving dog on the back porch and killed him, then they castrated him. My husband was livid. So was I.

I won't get into more details of anything. This was the start of one catastrophe after another. We had no peace in our home. People were barging in, and it was horrible.

Finally, when all the news came out, the police got pulled into this, not because of the preachers; they were going to resolve it all on their own, they said. Two young boys had other ideas. My husband ran away. The church took me by force out of my own home and made us live with another family. I was not allowed to go anywhere or do anything unless someone goes with me. I was not allowed to make any decisions. The children were a mess. One daughter screamed all the time, telling me how she hates me. She was only three years old. My little boy lost all his speech. He could do nothing anymore but scream. I felt helpless. I had no rights. I was never asked how I felt about anything. Now I was getting harassed day after day by the preachers. I have no idea how I survived.

My husband got arrested and put in jail. He got out on parole and came back to live in our house. Now the accusations started all over that I'm lying, that I'm secretly seeing this man. How could I? Where could I? I was being watched every minute. I was never allowed to sleep anywhere but with other people in their homes.

I didn't think I was being rebellious. I did every-thing they said; it was still not good enough. When my husband came back, he told them it was my fault. They immediately believed his stories, lies, and now they told me the shocking news that they are now putting me in the ban, the terrible word: *excommunication*. I was told by the preacher that they now cut me off from God. I am now on my way to hell, and I am not allowed to talk to my parents. If I do, they will inflict further punishment on me.

I was horrified. I still had one source of hope, my dad. I loved him. He kept pleading to the preachers for my case. This got turned on him. My parents' lives had turned upside down completely. Three daughters were gone. They had all been part of this awful happening. My youngest sister was nine when her tragedy started. I got beat down so bad; punishment after punishment got inflicted on me, the Bible jammed down my throat in the most horrendous way a person could have ever thought of.

The mother treated my children horribly, hitting them with big pieces of firewood. I would stand help-lessly by, watching this unfold. When they knew she was coming, they would go hide under the beds. She would eventually find them and beat them. She did it the most to my daughter. I was so numb, with shock and the tor-ture. I don't recall ever crying a tear. I held it all in. I had nobody to talk to. I got looked at with scorn and accused by everyone of what I have done, and now I'm being the horrible one in the community, how are we ever going to deal with telling other people? I was a total outcast, a reject, a bad, horrible, evil person. There was nothing good in me. Now I had to carry the shame of what my husband did, that it was all my fault.

I won't go into any more detail about this. I believe I have said enough to cause anyone some deep feelings to erupt. My parents got blamed for being bad parents, accused to no end. They got put out the church as a punishment. My dad was never the same. My parents looked like they had been beat down so badly; they never recovered. I like to say my dear dad died from a broken heart. He got dementia and died six years ago already. My mom is still alive.

Somehow, he managed to get me away from there with all the children. We escaped, and nobody knew where we were for two and half years. In the meantime, we had two more children. We got found, and my husband got arrested, and then he was sentenced a long prison sentence.

Being gone was the best thing that could have happened to me. I learned how to think. I was very bitter and angry. I learned that I didn't need those people. In their thinking, this is how we need to do things. They did the best they knew how. I'm sure they were scared.

All the people who told me to marry this man now came to me wringing their hands that they wish they would have never encouraged me to do this. What am I going to say? The damage was done. To me, he was still nicer than they were. At least he was kind and good to me; they sure weren't.

I was forced to move back to the community, moving in with my parents. That was the worst tragedy that could have ever happened. My baby, six weeks old, screamed all night long every night till he was a year old. He never slept. I took him to doctor after doctor. They found nothing. His back was so nutritionally deprived that every bone would be out of place. I had to take him to the chiropractor every week, sometimes twice a week. He screamed with earache constantly. We lived there one year with fifteen people in the house. My mom was so traumatized with us living there; she would throw herself on the kitchen floor and just start screaming, "Someone help me!" I would just stand there and stare at her, so angry and hateful at her. What could I do to help her?

God sent this amazing woman to live in the community with four children, having been divorced three times. Somehow, we started to connect, and I slowly started pouring my heart out to her. She also started talking to my sisters. She got us help to leave the community for counseling, a start of a new life.

In the process of all this, my one sister introduced me to a preacher and his wife, who helped people get saved and learn how to deal with their trauma. I wanted to go! I knew I needed something. My heart and soul were so hungry. For three weeks, they worked with me daily, praying me through to victory. First of all, I didn't even believe I was a sinner. How can I get past that? I like what a friend shared with me. She said, "Well, no, you didn't want or need to hear that yet. You already felt like the whole world was against you. Now God is too. I needed to hear I needed a Savior."

Letting go of all my hatred and bitterness toward my mom was the biggest, hardest thing. I could not understand the concept of allowing God into my heart. But God came in! He flooded my soul. My life has never been the same, will never be the same. I was like a newborn baby, hungry for milk and could never get enough.

I went back to my family and church, all excited, but they were angry. I was so puzzled. They were trying to change me. Now God has changed me. What is the problem?

Many, many more ugly things happened. I had no mentors to help grow me into a better person. After seven years of this ugliness, I finally said I'm done. I took the children and walked away. Only our clothes on our backs, no money, no home, no education, no job—just God, the children, and I.

I had no idea the trauma that would erupt from such abuse the children had been in emotionally, mentally, and in every way possible. I had to learn how to live for one. I had to learn how to be a human. God carried me many times. I have made many mistakes, but one thing is, I have never quit. I have never given up. I am a miracle survivor to say the least.

So many times I was so close to death, God miraculously brought me out. So many years, I was just surviving, nothing else. I still felt so crippled, in bondage, it holding me fast. The betrayal had taken a huge toll on me. I felt betrayed by my family, the church, and my husband. I'm praying on it that one sweet day, I can also write a book about how terrible this had impacted my health and how hard I've had to work to keep my health up.

In the last five years, I have grown more in my spiritual life than I ever did. When I desperately needed some help, I just did not know which way to turn. God sent me a messenger, a motivational speaker who has helped me grow immensely. My biggest struggle is to still deal with negativity.

Walking very closely with God is what helps me the most. I have the sweetest relationship with my mom. I shower her with love, hugs, and kisses, and I tell her how amazing she is. She is old and partly senile now, but before, her responses were always so negative, telling me she will only love me if I come back. I just blow it off.

I have learned to go back and be kind to everyone and treat them with love and respect. They don't have to like me, but like I told them many times, "You will learn to respect me. I accept nothing else."

This is how God has been breathing life into me. I love life. I appreciate life. I can talk about what happened and look at it, thinking with thanksgiving in my heart that I hold no grudges. I am not bitter. Sometimes I get emotional when I talk about certain things. I want the whole world to know, yes, we have a loving God. It wasn't God who did this; it was people who thought they need to be God. In all reality, they just did not know better.

Every day is a new journey for me. God has brought so many wonderful people into my life who help build me up, and they don't even know it! I appreciate every kind word. I cannot and will not take anything for granted. I value my life. I value people. I love to love people now.

There are so many more stories floating around in my mind. I realize I might need to write another book. Once again, I want to share, *this is my story*. I did not write it with intentions to hurt anyone else. I pray it can be a blessing. Learning how to be a positive role model for my children is also very important for me right now.

"The picture I sent of me is a reminder of happiness and peace and joy amidst extreme hardship. Three months to the day after finishing my story, my daughter whom I wrote about in the book having been born with heart problems, Deborah, took her own life with a gun to her head in her own kitchen. Deborah moved back home two years ago to start her life over from all the horrible trauma she had experienced as a child and into adulthood, which led her to become a full-fledged alcoholic. She celebrated her two-year sobriety two days before her death and ended her life one day short of two years moving back. She had a vision of sharing her story worldwide. And we shared many hours of dreaming and planning. She left three letters behind. She could not live her life anymore. The pain was too deep, too many tragedies had happened, and she could not dull her pain any longer. The grief of losing a daughter to our already pain-filled life is more than I can bear, but I have a vision, and God showed me that I must share her story. She is gone, but her life story will remain forever."

ABOUT THE AUTHOR

With great pleasure do I finish my book about my painful, lonely life as a child and into my adult years. I am so grateful that I can take others into the story of my life to share the pain and trauma, not because I want pity or be put into a victim box, but I want to shout out to the world for everyone to know that regardless what hurdles life may throw at us, we can be cleansed from all the ugliness, the bitterness and receive a clean new heart! Forgiveness can be so painful to let go but so empowering, so cleansing to the soul.

I am so very touched that the publishers accepted my book. I cannot even begin to express the joy I feel, the freedom and the empowerment it gives me! Because I see that there is hope for me, I can really and truly do more than just survive. I can thrive! It is my joy to be able to share my story with others for that very reason. I believe thousands and millions will be touched and even experience a life change because of what I wrote.

God led me through every part of this book. Some were so painful, I was nearly screaming in pain as I felt the gut-wrenching story come out of my being. When I was done, the change over me was so powerful. I felt cleansed from so much garbage. Now it is my desire to walk even closer with God and see what the next part of my journey will be. My deepest blessings and love to each individual who reads these words. Remember, you are not alone.